by YAYA

1

~ to love is to live

Beneath My Skin

Poetry By Yaya

Beneath My Skin / YAYA BATES

ISBN: 9798418693600

Printed in United Kingdom

BOOK DESIGN, COVER DESIGN AND PHOTOGRAPHY BY YAYA

Photography credit: Simon Bartholomew

Beneath My Skin

Dear David

Sending you lots of love 3 Elizabeth! Hope you enjoy my poetry, pictures & prose.

With love,

Yaya xx.

I hope you enjoy the collection of poems, pictures and prose in my debut book. If you want to follow me on social media, you can find me on IG at **poetrybyyaya**. Here you will find links to other social media platforms, all accessible from my profile.

For business enquiries, please visit my website at:

www.thoughtsbyyaya.com

Or email me directly at: **info@thoughtsbyyaya.com**

Yaya is a writer, poet and spoken-word performer. She is also a qualified marketing professional, having gained her DipM from the Chartered Institute of Marketing in 2000. She has over two decades of experience in marketing.

She has worked in various roles in the public and private sector, including a long-held post as the Senior Communications & Marketing Manager for BBC Radio & Music, before becoming a director and co-owner of a creative agency specialising in marketing and design services for corporate events.

Yaya has also been a radio presenter and DJ for a local community radio station, TFS Radio, presenting two, three-hour weekly radio shows.

Yaya spent her formative years' training for a career as a classical ballet dancer at the National Theatre Ballet School, in Melbourne, Australia, under the tutelage of Anne Jenner (Principal of The Royal Ballet), the late Gailene Stock (Director of The Royal Ballet School) and Gary Norman

(Senior Ballet Master, Royal Ballet School). She was accepted into the prestigious Western Australian Academy of Performing Arts.

Still, she turned it down after receiving a place in Sydney at the Glenn Street Academy of Performing Arts (incorporating Sydney City Ballet).

Unfortunately, an injury to her right foot requiring multiple surgeries cut short her performance career in classical ballet. Still, the performer in her has never retired.

Once a performer, always a performer!

here is no north without south, up without down, high without low, and day without night. And so it follows that there can be no happiness without sadness. Life is beautiful, but it is also tragic!

Bad things happen - they always do. They have happened to me many times in my life, and I anticipate that they will probably happen many more times before I exit this world. Sometimes I feel I have had more than my fair share. They were not deserved or caused by any failings on my part. They were random; they did not choose me, and I certainly did not select them. It was merely a case of bad luck. But I continue to survive. Why? Because there is always something to live for and the possibility that tomorrow will be a better day.

Even though I have felt that I am flying into the wind, pushing back against the forces of nature and the forces of bad luck, I have somehow managed to find the strength to keep moving forward no matter what. No matter how large the battle appeared or how distant success may have seemed, I have kept going. Writing

has helped me during the many lows and the highs
of life; it has helped me with self-expression, and it
has also helped me heal myself and rediscover joy
after periods of intense grief. There is something so
powerful about putting one's thoughts down on paper
and something even more potent in sharing them with
others. It makes me feel accountable, but also in sharing
them, I have discovered that I am certainly not alone in
many of these life experiences.

This poetry book is a collection of poems penned
over the last few years. I hope you find love, hope,
inspiration or strength of your own from my words. We
can choose to move towards the people who bring us
light; we can also be the light source for others.

Thank you for purchasing a copy of this book. The
book can be opened at any point and read in any
order. I have deliberately avoided putting the poems in
chronological order, as I do not view life as linear!

Love, YAYA x

Even though I say
I ought not to force
myself into your life

I still find myself looking
for the smallest opening
even the tiniest gap

Where I can
squeeze myself in

Should I start at the start

or should I skip to the end?

There is so much to impart

are you ready, my friend?

Now hold on real tight

it might get pretty rough

But you're welcome to leave

if you've heard quite enough

Now, this story is not fiction

No, this story is fact!

Still, it is not the full story

just merely an extract

As an Instagram poet, I have always used the captions section to context my thoughts behind each piece further. I have therefore selected to do the same here in my debut book. Poems have different meanings for different people, so by all means, if you see something else in my words, then you were most likely meant to see it. These are simply my thoughts about life and what I have learnt as a mother of four, living abroad for most of my adult life, how I have come to terms with a career-ending injury and battling anorexia as a teenager. My coping mechanisms from the effects of an abusive step-father and trying to make it through the terrible loss of a child. I have worked in the creative fields of dance, music and design, human resources and marketing and communications. These thoughts are merely my perspective and my reality. I hope you can relate to a few of my ideas or perhaps many more. Thank you for buying this book, and for taking the time to read my words. I am truly grateful.

There is
a feeling
bubbling up
inside of me
ready to explode

It's churning
and I'm yearning
to one day
let it go

We all want to feel beautiful and find someone who appreciates our outer beauty and recognises our inner beauty. Someone who will see 'beneath our skin' and accept us for who we truly are. And despite our many flaws and evident human failings, find someone who will prioritise and love us as a whole person without shame, guilt, or judgement.

What makes you feel beautiful? A person or a passion? A friend or a lover? Has there been a time in your life when you have never felt more beautiful?

I feel beautiful when I am smiling and genuinely happy. I feel beautiful when I am dancing, singing, writing or creating. I feel beautiful when surrounded by my friends and family, who make me laugh aloud and fill me with blissful joy.

I feel beautiful when I feel valued and rewarded for my work and when friends make time, in their busy schedules, to see me or talk with me. I feel beautiful when they patiently listen to anything I have to say, which is usually a lot!

I have never felt more beautiful

since I caught your eye

I have never felt more beautiful

or happier inside

I have never felt more beautiful

than under your gaze

I have never felt more beautiful

in all of my days

I stumble as I write

for you are not mine alone

and hesitate to share

all that is unbeknown

Yet, compelled I somehow feel

to find the words to show

how you always fill my heart

until I overflow

Perhaps, we should only ever whisper some words in the ear of those closest enough to hear.

Sharing our private thoughts, hopes, and dreams can sometimes make us feel they are no longer ours.

In the process of sharing them, they have unintentionally become a commodity and owned no longer by you or me. Yet still, I will write these words for all to see.

For there is some comfort in knowing and seeing that these feelings, even if fleeting, were once real.

When I lost it

I looked for it

I willed it

back to me

I knew that

I had found it

when in our eyes

we both could see

(joy)

Within me

within me

inside you'll

forever be

The memory

of our love

looping

(interminably)

What does 'yes' feel like for you? When do you get the
sense that something is right for you? For me, it's never
a difficult decision but simply a feeling, an intuition. An
internal mantra is chanting away about the future I'd like
to see for me. Look at the things you admire in others. Is
it their creativity? Their spirit? Their passion for the arts?
Their love of music? Their unwavering conviction? Their
conscientiousness? Their compassion? Their humour? Or
perhaps it is their energy and the light they bring when they
enter a room.

The way they make you feel about yourself? Their soft look
and kind eyes? Their gentle nature? Their ability to make
everyone feel important, loved and worthy? These are the
things that 'yes' feels like to me—never forced—never sold—
never waiting to be told that this is right (for me). We need
to know ourselves well enough to know what we need to
do to live our life without any regrets. To understand what
genuinely turns us on and will genuinely make us happy.
'Yes' is knowing what enough means for us and how to fill
the void when we feel we may not have enough. What will
enough be? What will it look like when we have enough?

'Yes'

Feels like perfect intuition
never a difficult decision

Never forced, never sold
never waiting to be told
that this is right

(for me)

I realise there is no hope for me. There is no turning back. I've crossed that threshold. You know, the one where you no longer feel anything for anyone, other than the one you love!

Where you've no desire to look for anyone else and no desire to seek

a different face
a different smile
a different voice

You've already made your choice. And you look at others, and you feel, or more to the point, you don't 'feel' anything! That's my point.

It is only you that I keep returning to...

There are times when you have to make a decision and go with a feeling. You've got to go with what feels right. It may not always make sense to you or those around you. It may make people question your motives or may even make people question your mind.

But sometimes, you have a feeling. And this feeling is one of a kind. Who is to say you're mistaken and that perhaps others are right. Why not explore the potential opportunity and let your intuition guide you.

I've always understood
that feelings come, and feelings go
I know this to be true, as they usually do
Yet, somehow this is not the case
when it comes to you

When it comes to you, they seem to stay
I wonder how I seem to wake each day
and still, feel exactly the same way

(about you)

To know oneself is an outstanding achievement, as it means that we are genuinely in tune with how we feel, which can help us to empathise with others. It can help us to recognise that our emotions are often only temporary and emotions that stay are perhaps ones that require a little more attention/exploration.

But how do you, or how can you, ever honestly know if another feels the same way about you? Reciprocity is always the biggest fear in any relationship. Will it work, will it last and will they like me as much as I like them? It's easy to know oneself, but it is much more complex and often takes longer to get to know another.

Do you know what they dream of, what they want? Can you put yourself in their shoes for a minute and truly empathise with all they are going through. Would you support them in their dreams? Would you help them when they are down? Your intuition may guide you, but it, too, needs time for exploration.

Take things slow and see how it goes.

Live in the moment! The past is the past! Don't make it last, too long!

The pages are turned
at the start of each day
A new page to write
with new things to say
And like a story is read
from beginning to end
When a new day begins
I always try to unsend

(what has gone)

Do not speak to me

We are at the stage

where...

a look, a sigh

a breath, a smile

conveys more

than words

will ever say

(I feel you)

Even as an IG poet who loves the digital landscape, there is no real substitute for physical contact. There is no substitute for spending quality time with the person or people we love and adore and soaking up the joyful feeling, the energy, the chemistry and the vibrations that one gets from being close to the person or the people we love.

It may seem strange coming from a poet, but communicating without words always feels more honest. More sensual. More human. Allowing our bodies to let go and respond naturally to the cosmic energy that emanates from another feels more authentic. Allowing our eyes to speak for us and convey all we need to say feels more human. In this digital world, we need to try and remain as human as possible.

I wonder about you most days and if you are okay. I wonder
what you're up to and what you're busy doing. I imagine
you are absorbed in your passion. I imagine you are losing
track of time. I then wonder if someone made you smile
today. And if they did, I wonder who it was. I then wonder
if perhaps it was thinking of me that made you smile. Then I
wonder if I have even crossed your mind today.

Or perhaps it was you who made yourself smile. Maybe you
are your source of joy. I imagine that you are. I then wonder
why it is that I wonder so much about you. I wonder why I'm
so curious about you. I then wonder what makes me wonder.
Perhaps it is because I think you are truly wonderful. Yes,
maybe this is true. Maybe I love you. Yes, perhaps I do.

I wonder, as I lay here
and my imagination travels far
I wonder, as I lay here
if you are happy where you are

I wonder, as I lay here
as wonder is all that I can do
Only wonder and imagine
who might be lying next

(to you)

I see it

and I wonder

I ask myself why you do

Why is it that you wear

my gift I gave to you

You must like it

or is it more than that

I wish I only knew

I wonder if you wear it

for the same reason that

(I do)

It's hard to be rational when one feels governed by their emotions and allows them to dominate the decision. We often veer towards people who boost or soothe our ego and look for ideas that confirm our beliefs. We think we are rational and in control of our emotions but do not appreciate how easily we can let someone change our perspective with a gentle push, especially if we are leaning towards this belief anyway. The more challenging option is to challenge one's ego and apply a rational view rather than a selfish one. We can delay judgment or action until our strong emotions no longer influence us.

It is easy to sabotage relationships and ruin a good thing when we act impulsively, allowing emotions to cloud our vision. Deliberate for longer and delay, as it is difficult to take back our words once said. When we make a decision, we seek allies to confirm the decision we made was the right one, even if we discover later it was not! How often do we try and justify our choices to ourselves and others? It's a constant battle with our ego and aversion to loss! Make a decision, and you will often find it hard to undo! It's true.

Pure intentions

turned on their head

Every piece now tainted

by what you have said

Every line penned

every word of it was true

Still, you found it hard to believe

I could ever fall in love

(with you)

Our dreams are where we escape the day and have the
opportunity to live an alternative life to the one that we
are living in our waking day. Some may see their dreams
as fantasy, but how can we be confident that they are not
another form of reality. One where we are free to be who we
truly want to be. One where we see the people we want to
see. Dream on, dreamer.

I dream about love
and I love all my dreams
If I love you, I will tell you
in my dreams you were seen

She's looking in the mirror
all her senses are now numb
She looks in disbelief
at the person, she has become

The mirror is her best friend
and reflects what others see
It was the one that whispered to her
it's now time that you were

(free)

42

I like to look at the timeline of people's profile pictures on Facebook. The profile pics of a particular woman fascinated with mirrors caught my attention. As the years went by, I noticed that she appeared more and more distressed in the pictures she was taking in the mirror. This poem is about her, but it could be about anyone.

I hope she is finally free of whatever it was that was making her unhappy. I know that feeling well. Happiness comes from freedom, but it takes a lot of courage to be free.

I'm so mad at you

but I'm madder at me

Still, I am mad at you

as mad as can be

But I'm calming down

as I am starting to see

I am only mad at you

for saying that you

(loved me)

My smile does not belong to you
it is mine; it comes from me
For a while, I thought
it came from you
but this smile is owned by me

My smile is what I give to you
especially when you are kind
But my smile will
always belong to me
this smile you see

(is mine)

Into you, into me

feeling it grow deeper

in intensity

Into you, I now want to climb

exploring your depths

as you explore mine

Into me, I now let you come

there is no denying

that you are the one

(for me)

Trust your intuition and your inner voice; it is there as your guide. If we trust our intuition, it will likely protect us from harm and unfavourable outcomes. It will often help us make the right decisions and choices that sit more comfortably with who we are or want to be. Options that are often in our best interest and will serve us well.

There are times we may not feel all that 'into' what we are doing, or perhaps where we are going. What once might have made us feel good may no longer make us feel so great. But when it feels right, we know. We feel it in the air. We feel it everywhere. We feel wonderfully light, and life is no longer a fight.

Know yourself well enough to trust your intuition. Let it guide you. Feel it, recognise it, and believe it.

Sometimes we look for our happiness in others! By this, I mean that we often willingly give other people the power to give or take away our smiles. We allow others to affect our mood. To jeopardise our day! But the reality is, only we have the power to take our happiness away! How?

Believing others are responsible for our smile and their actions will dictate our happiness. While a smile from another can be fantastic too, don't forget that smiling can also be a smile for you. When I look in the mirror, I smile, you see, because I like the person looking back at me!

She was

a light

that scattered

and spread

from holes

in her armour

where once

she had bled

You are the only one

who truly sees me

and the only one with

whom I desire to be

(truly seen)

Inspired by your light, obsessed with your flame, a force that's so strong, it returns again and again? Some say that love is the real bond between us, but what fans both our flames will always be pure lust! There's no denying that a muse flames the coals of our forbidden desires.

Generated by the soul, it is a spiritual energy that is often difficult to control. Sustained by the unavailability and kept alive by mystery, lust has been the real glue between a man and woman throughout history.

When the urge is strong
it's difficult to explain
how the desire returns
again and again

My body takes over
as my mind has one aim
to only seek what it needs
in love and lust's name

He was not one to shout when you were already standing near. He would instead prefer to whisper something softly in your ear. He would rather listen to hear what you have to say. He would rather listen for the whole entire day! Just to make you smile!

With words so few
so uniquely you
and a tick that turned
from grey to blue

(I love you)

Could it be

the simplest memory

that still keeps me

(holding on)

A tender movement

to show you care

a delicate sweep of my hair

(from my face)

A simple action

etched in my mind

a memory of the last time

(we were together)

Little control

an involuntary act

A powerful force

keeps pulling

me back

(to you)

When you are in tune with your mind, body and soul, you will find that you instinctively know what to do. Look for the signs and try and listen for the clues, as often your body will know what is best for you.

Chemistry is everything, and we are attracted to people for the same reason that the roots of a tree will find their way to the water. They feel a vibration, then listen for the sound, and when they are in tune with their environment, their nourishment is found.

When your roots call out for each other, they will find a way to be intertwined. What comes naturally is what we often enjoy the most. Follow the path of least resistance.

Ear to the ground

I listened intently

for any sound

For a sign that

you were

coming

I waited, with a smile

I laid there for a while

I had truly believed

that you were

(coming)

It shaped her

it pushed her

it helped her to see

It gave her the courage

to tell the world

(this is me)

I remember sitting on the bathroom floor with you; our legs splayed across the floor. Both were in awe of the passion that had gone before. I remember the way you looked at me as you said, 'Look at you!' And I replied with 'What do you mean?'

You had this wonderful look in your eyes like you had won first prize! I fell in love with that man. The one who thought I was amazing. I wish I could find him again. I do not know where he has gone.

A tender hand
upon my face
Our legs now splayed
across the floor

As he looked deep
into my soul
I knew he was
all I'd been

(looking for)

What could be more tender than a gentle caress of your face or loving fingers through your hair? The tenderness, gentleness, and kindness that comes after the throws of passion will show you how much they care. These are the signs to look for, the possible signs of true love.

Eyes that followed
eyes that met
It was a moment in time
we would never regret

Eyes that offered
eyes that gave
It was a moment in time
we both had craved

Today

my closet

felt bare

For all I wanted

to wear

(was you)

The difficulties and challenges we face are catalysts for achieving great things. People will try and stop you as you try to escape from the clutches of mediocrity. They'll tell you that you should settle. They'll tell you that you should stay humble. They'll tell you that you should be grateful for what you have and feel ashamed for wanting more. They'll tell you that it's okay to be average all your life - a 'jack of all trades' and master of none. They'll tell you that life's not a competition and that you should avoid competing. Then they'll say to you to be silent, simply so that they can speak! They'll let you know these are all virtues, but they are only vices for the weak.

I found myself wanting
wanting, what might be
I found you amidst the chaos
or was it you, who did find me?

Where desire led to wanting
and the wanting led to you
A silent truth between us
a truth our souls both knew

I want to love you until

you feel the breathlessness I do

I want to love you until

you fall in love with me too

I want to love you until

you feel the oceans of fatigue

I want to love you until

you fall down on your knees

and surrender

(to me)

How many days do I remember?

How many hours do I recall?

I not only remember every minute

I remember every second

of it all

(with you)

Quality consistently over quantity. When time is precious, how do you choose to spend the hours of your day? And when time is scarce, how are you choosing to use the minutes and the seconds of your day. Suppose you were only granted a minute each week in the company of those you love. What would you do? Or what would you choose to say in those precious sixty seconds?

I practice this exercise over and over. It focuses the mind on the critical activity for me to do that day. It urges me to be bold and to say what it is that I want to say. Tomorrow is not a given, so it's a good habit to think about what you will do with your day's seconds and minutes instead of the hours. You'll start to appreciate how little time we all have to do what we want to do and say what we want to say.

It has to be mutual

you have to be sure

It has to leave you wanting

wanting so much more

(of me)

It has to be mutual, and you have to be sure, and they have to leave you longing for more. There needs to be chemistry, and there needs to be fun. There needs to be the feeling that they are the one.

It has to feel natural. It has to feel free. So please do not lose yourself if you fall in love with me. Keep yourself true. Keep doing what you do. If you do, you can be sure I will fall in love with you too.

I could try and explain myself

but it'll probably come out wrong

I could say it's because I love you

but I've been saying it for so long

I could try and explain why seeing you

with others fills me with such envy

But it's hard for me when I see them

in the place I long to be

I could pretend I'm okay not seeing you

and an emoji is enough

But we both know that anything

other than face-to-face is pretty tough

It's not easy, and I admit

I struggle in many ways and

I'm sorry for pushing you into a corner

where you felt you had to say

"I love you'

I'm sorry! But I needed to hear it,

even if it wasn't to my face

I needed to know, I needed to hear

I had a special place

I've tried to cope with the moments

and few words we do exchange

But it's not easy when I'm waiting

for all of this to change

It's not easy I admit

this wanting more of you

It's hard to be in love

when I cannot have

(all of you)

Loss aversion is one of our greatest battles. We fight it with all our might! We kick and scream as we pull ourselves away. We feel our grip tighten and beg for it to stay! But we often know that we have to let go!

I showed her to my mother
who took one look and said

My darling daughter now listen
not to your heart, but to your head
I brought you up with courage
I brought you up to know
there are some things worth keeping
but there are some things you must

(let go)

Safety felt in numbers

even if it's only two

Playing silly games

all because of you

When people choose to play games with you, you have two choices: either participate in the game or remove yourself from the situation. It takes two to tango, and there's no need to enter into a game that you're not interested in playing! Self-respect is appreciating your true worth by avoiding interactions with those looking for a reaction. Please do not give them any satisfaction.

A mind of its own
as if it belongs to you

And though I try to calm it
there is nothing I can do

To stop myself believing
in a love that feels

(so true)

The human brain loves to love - it does! It releases happy hormones when we are in love! We all love to feel good, and being in love is possibly the best feeling in the world!

Why is love initially easy yet much more complex and demanding as we go? Why does love become more challenging the more we ask to know?

Is it not simply enough to believe that the love you feel is true? Is it not enough when they say the words; I love you, I really do!

It used to feel so very simple
there was no need to explain

Now it seems so far from simple
that we will never be the same

(again)

I'm so very tired of texting

when all I want is you

The virtual world for me

I'm afraid will no longer do!

(I love you)

The insanity of staring into a screen when all I really want is
you! I've now reached my limits where the virtual world will
no longer do! Have you?

We often think we want more! More opportunities to explore. More chances to see what is behind the next door. But sometimes, there is nothing more to see. Nothing more than curiosity!

Many is what so many want
not just one, for it is too few
One, even if near perfect
for many, would not do

Many is what I think of when I think
of what you might choose
One, even if near perfect
in love they still might lose

Many is what so many want
still, some are happy with just one
Even if they are far from perfect
it is far better than having

(none)

A kiss is

not a contract

but please tell that

to my heart

that swore it would

love no other

the moment

our lips did part

Being in love with love might seem like criticism, but perhaps it is merely an observation of your ability to love! It's all a matter of perspective, and whether you're a true romantic at heart? Do you like to surprise your loved ones with unexpected gifts, little love notes or small gestures to show that you care? Most artists, musicians and poets are in love with love? Would Al Green and James Brown have been successful if they spoke about hate? If Al told you to give up on the idea of love and happiness! If he told you not to stay together?

After all, artists generally sell the concept of love through our music, words, paintings, and stories we tell in theatre and on film. Most people capitalise on it! But I genuinely believe in it! Some of us like to think that we will find the one who will be a perfect match. Is that so wrong? I don't think it is wrong, and I don't believe anyone else does either. Do you?

You said,

I'm in love with love

and maybe that's true

But I'm not simply

in love with love

I'm only in love

(with you)

Perfect

was a pedestal

you put me on easily

How disappointed

you now appear

perfection is

(not me)

We sometimes like to believe that someone out there is perfect, or perhaps simply perfect for us. Yet, it is a fantasy to think someone can exist without flaws. That they will not make mistakes or, at some point, disappoint us. When we put people on a pedestal, we are putting them out of reach! We tell them they are beyond us, above us, or better than us. We may idolise, admire or even love them. But often, they are lonely up there on the pedestal that you have put them, knowing sooner or later you will have to bring them down!

Sooner or later, they will find out that you are not perfect after all! You are not amazing! You are just you! And when they do, you also know it will be your fault that they are no longer in love with you. I don't want to be perfect, amazing, or legendary. All I want to do is exist in this world like me!

When you are indeed in love, you can't imagine the same passion with anyone else. But do you ever wonder if anyone else before you felt the same kind of love that you feel for them now?

No two loves are ever the same, and there are different levels of love. The love we have for our friends, family members or children is one type of love. But the love that we might experience for another (our true love) is something entirely different! Something truly magical!

Is she like me?

I wonder, I do

Did she feel the same way

that I do, with you?

I often wonder

if the way that I feel

when I am with you

is the same kind of love

that she has felt too?

Is she like me?

I often wonder, I do

If she felt the same way

that I do, with you?

(I love you)

My dreams are full of you...

Getting more vivid

getting more real

these dreams of you

I can almost feel

The touch of your hand

the scent of your skin

the warmth of your breath

as you pull me in

(close to you)

When we feel safe, that we belong and that we matter, it triggers an emotional state that motivates us to perform, create, innovate and move forward. Safety is essential, so is a sense of belonging! But being publicly acknowledged by someone you love is perhaps the most powerful for me!

When they tell the world that you matter to them, that you are perfect to them, and for them, in my eyes, they are proving that they want it to last!

When you live in the moment

not the future, nor the past

You have only this moment

to prove you want it

(to last)

How do you know if they love you? It's easy! You can feel it in their kiss!

Do you love me?

Do you love me?

Oh, please tell me so

I love you dear Yaya

but first I'll put on a show

I'll do it in public

for my best friends to see

I'll announce that I love you

when you're standing behind me!

Do we need an invitation, or should we invite ourselves in?
Is the door now wide open, or will it close again? Hearing
the words is helpful when you're unsure of what to do, but it
is always the look within their eyes that is the most obvious
clue if you should stay!

A meeting or just a greeting
a 'how you doing' or just a 'hi'

A 'please come a little closer'
a look you see in their eyes

(to please stay)

I like the unanticipated, the unforeseen. I enjoy discovery of
all I have not seen. I like the unknown, the feeling of chance.
I enjoy the unpredictability of love's long dance, with you!

I like the unexpected

the same way that you do

The surprising , the sudden

the impulsive out of the blue

I like the unexpected

the same way that you do

The staggering, the startling

the way it always feels brand new

(with you)

If you believe you are in love, it's most likely that you are, for who are we but what we think! And while loving someone that you can't have or who doesn't love you in return can satisfy a need to love, the magic only really happens when they feel as lucky to have encountered you as you do to have discovered them.

You can't always find love when you look for it, but you can undoubtedly recognise it when it finds you. When you feel it, you will know. Suddenly everything seems to make sense.

Am I getting warmer? Can you feel it too? The flame is growing bigger, the closer I get to you!

I search for you under bridges
I look for you in the trees

I try my best to find you
so that one day we can be

(together)

Our wardrobe communicates to others who we are, but it can also serve as a reminder of who we once were! It can sum up our values, competence, confidence, innocence, independence, and who we desire to be.

When someone asks you what you are going to wear, they show a genuine interest in who you are. What will I wear today? Well, I'm glad you asked!

It is not merely a piece of fabric
It is not only something to wear
It is the simple fact you asked me
that shows how much you really care

(who I am)

How do you know it's love? How do you know it's true? It is simply this. If you truly love someone, then what hurts them will hurt you too.

It was the first time I had seen
you write these words
and I cried, as one might do

I cried because
I loved your words,
and what hurts you hurts me

(too)

The answer is in the question?

People often ask me
to describe how it will feel
when you've found your true love
How will you know if it's real?

Well, the question itself
is the answer, indeed
for true love is not a question
and there is no answer you will need

(to hear)

If I write it down, does it make it more true? If I express in words how I feel about you?

I would rather not write
I would rather you see
I would rather you felt it
when you were looking

(at me)

What is your love language?

I have not run out of words

to say

I still have plenty

left for you

I simply want to show you

another way

How much I really do

(love you)

I like to read back through messages and comments received and words that have meant a lot to me. These days I find I am doing it a lot more than I have done in the past. I use Snapchat occasionally to message friends, but unfortunately, my words disappear on this app unless either of us chooses to save them in the chat! I like this form of communication when I'm chatting to friends daily; however, when the conversations are less frequent, I prefer to message using other apps to allow me to reread their words. Sometimes when I wake in the middle of the night, I will grab these words and hold them tight! There is something about rereading words that came out right!

A new kind of love
a love that is typed
Words we hold close
when alone at night

Here was pure poetry

you could see it in her eyes

An unwavering conviction

never needing to

question why

(she loved him)

There is something about the steadiness, the conviction and the belief one has, not only in oneself but in another person. One does not need to question their commitment or love of the other and is confident to wait, safe in the knowledge that their search is over. One is happy within themselves to know that they are truly enough.

How long should we hold on to a memory of a magnificent moment? It's easy to feel the addictive pull of the incredible high. It's much harder to wave these moments goodbye. But we must bid them farewell and look for the new. There are many more moments that are waiting for you. Find them. The world is waiting.

Drenched in the moment
I wrung myself dry
It was merely a moment
a magnificent high

Merely a moment
in time and with you
A moment to remember
yet one to forget too

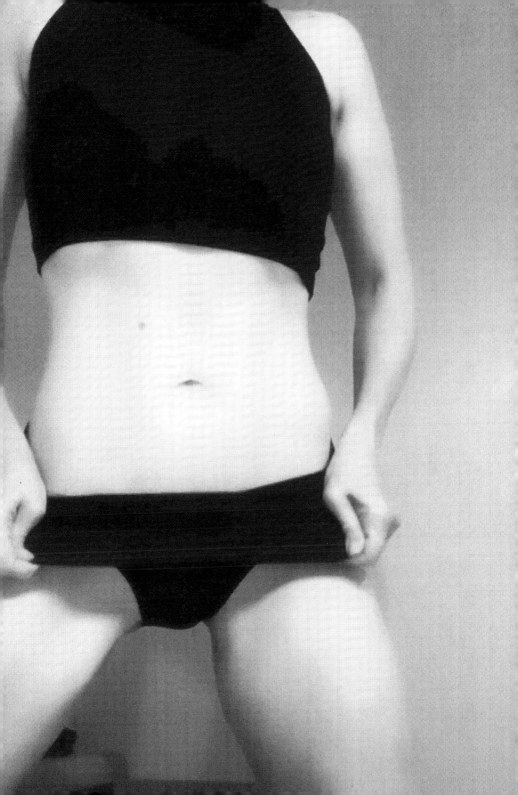

When you get a moment
a moment when you are free
I am not asking for a lifetime
or expecting eternity

But if you get a moment
a moment when you are free
I'd like it if you could spend
this precious moment

(with me)

It is hard to admit that one is lonely. To say it out loud! As though one should be ashamed or embarrassed to accept such a thing! I enjoy the solitude! Some days I crave it! And yet loneliness is perhaps the biggest epidemic we face in modern society! Loneliness impacts our health in so many ways, including but not limited to our sleep quality and our mental health!

People may pretend they are not lonely, but everyone will experience loneliness at some point in their life! I try and give as much of my time to everyone, regardless of who they are! I understand that a kind word or a kind gesture can make all the difference when one is lonely and enduring periods of isolation! If you are a non-lonely person, try and spare a moment for someone who might be.

I no longer have
dark days anymore
I no longer feel
the way I did before

The days I have now
since the day that we met
are the days I shall remember
the only days I won't forget

(are with you)

Fishing! I loved fishing as a child! I would take my reels
and rods out onto the pier in Yarrawonga or Corowa
and sit for hours with my brothers hoping for a rainbow
trout, but often only managing to catch the greedy
bottom feeders, which were the Murray carp! They were
big, but they were tasteless as they fed on the mud at the
bottom of the Murray River. The trout, however, was
much harder to catch!

It was not greedy like the carp and would only ever
nibble at the bait, never taking a large bite as the carp
did. If I did manage to catch a trout, and it was small, I
would always set it free, throwing it back into the river.
But oh, how I loved its shiny rainbow scales. And even
though it was more beautiful than all the other fish and
I admired it, I knew it was not ready for me.

And though there is always plenty of fish in the sea (or
river as the case may be), there is no other fish that is
quite like me, or YOU!

There may be plenty

of fish in the sea

but there's no other

fish that is quite like

(me)

You could dream it

or wish for it

or hope for it

to come true

But the only way

you will find it

is when it

finds you

(love)

Being restricted or contained or no longer having the freedom to be, do or see what we always want is incredibly difficult. Still, we can focus on the things that we can change or focus on what we can't! At an early age, I learnt how to escape when I was beginning to feel trapped. I'd close my eyes and try to visualise a place where I felt at peace! I would use the power of my imagination and my memory of the happy times to take me back to these moments! And even to this day, I still do this! I still use visualisation to recall my most incredible experiences. To remind me of the things I want to achieve and would like to experience again.

I am aware that I have the power to choose what I want to see! I can block out painful memories, or I can choose to bring them back into my consciousness. I know that terrible things happen, but we can either let them destroy us or find a way to prosper from them! Everything is subjective! Absolutely everything is perception. Choose to see the positives in life, and you choose to be happy! Nothing is happening to us; it is only ever happening within us!

Where I am today

is not where I wish to be

but it is not where I am that matters

when I can always choose

what I will see

For when I close my eyes

I am where I wish to be

I am in your arms

I am kissing you

and you are

(kissing me)

The world is a vast place! There are over seven and a half billion people on the planet, which means that there is a possibility there could be ten thousand others who might be waiting for you! It's possible, and it's true!

So out of these seven and a half billion people, there will always be more than one person in this world who may be right for you! I doubt I will even meet a few! I doubt that you will too.

Even if I did, I still believe. I am still convinced. I could never love them the way that I love you!

There could be ten thousand others

it's possible, it's true

There could be ten thousand more

that might make me feel

the way you do

But if by chance I met them all

or even just a few

I know there would be no other

I would ever love

the way that

(I love you)

Will' 'love' wait forever! I read a lovely piece shared on a fellow poet's story. It was an excerpt by author Lemony Snickett that began with, 'I will love you if I never see you again, and I will love you if I see you every Tuesday, then a lot more I love you's - like the pepperoni loves the pizza etc. It ends with, I will love you if you marry someone else—and I will love you if you never marry at all, and spend your years wishing you had married me after all. That is how I will love you even as the world goes on its wicked ways.' And so the world has been in 2020 and even more so in 2021. And the world may be having its wicked ways with us all, but I believe that if love is to last, it must be able to ride the waves of the good times with the bad and the happy with the sad. And if they are the one, if they are indeed the one, then they will wait for you! They will wait for that message in a bottle!

Will it ever end
or forever will it be
this love I feel for you
and this love you feel for me

I know not of the answer
only of what I wish to be
For this love to last forever
for you to forever be

(with me)

You know how to calm

the storm in you

and how to calm

the same storm

in me

A kind of peace that comes

from a love that is true

believing we are

(meant to be)

Do you feel at peace with them? Do they help you calm
the storm within! Or do they make you feel uncertain,
unsteady and no longer sure-footed? Are you trying to
steady yourself constantly, or do they hold your hand
and tell you to look at the horizon?

A loving relationship is finding inner peace with
someone who brings you happiness, helps you feel calm
and knows how to keep the fire lit and the passion alive!
Where the majority of the time, 'All is good!'

I have a sinking feeling

a feeling that I fear

A feeling you may feel

whenever I am near

A feeling that might frighten

or make you run away

The feeling of being in love

but not knowing

if you should say

(I love you too)

Some things seem to get better with age! Items that are

no longer brand new but are still loved and cherished as if

they are. And you still feel the same excitement that you

did the very first time you laid eyes on it, or perhaps them!

You still look at it, or possibly them, with the same wonder,

with the same awe. And as it ages and is worn, it takes on

an appearance that reflects all it has experienced! You can

now see the scuffs and the cracks, and perhaps areas that no

longer have their shine, but these matter not, as you have

loved it for a long time! And just like an old vinyl or a well-

loved and well-read book, it is more about the way that it

feels, not the way that it looks!

They can make you feel at peace and can make you feel at ease! But it only takes one little look, and you are suddenly weak at the knees. And as you try to recover yourself, ever so swiftly, they smile as they leave you wondering how they make your heart beat so quickly!

When I won

the wishbone wish

I did not wish for thee

I wished what I knew

would be a wish for you

which was a wish to be

(happy)

Oh, love. It is such a tremendous feeling that we so desperately want to stay, but it can also be a feeling that may make us want to run away.

As humans, we try and do our best to avoid any situation or circumstance that might cause us pain. As a result, we may even give up our passions or forget our dreams; instead, taking a comfortable job in a safe industry. We may opt for a safe and mediocre life without the intensity or the fire.

But a life without love is undoubtedly a life that we soon will tire of.

Surprised you

always seem

as though you

cannot see

How it is

I've come to

love you

How I still wish

for you to be

(with me)

And the wonder always stays, and you still look at each other in awe. Out of all the people in the world, how is it that you came walking through my door? How is it that you love me, the way that I love you? How is it that I want you and that you still want me too?

A mutual attraction is what we wish upon a star. Someone who will love us, just the way we are!

Positive energy heading in the direction you want to go, and there's nothing you want more than to go with the flow! The feeling of always wanting to come back for more, as though there is always something new to explore.

The longing feeling that always stays. The excitement that never seems to go away! You want to see them from every angle and to see them from every view. And you know from their look, they feel the same way too!

You see it in their gaze. The eyes that declare they want you to stay! When focused on the one you desire, you cannot tear yourself away!

Perhaps it would

be easier to lie

To say that

it is not true

But the sheer length of time

and all the signs

Show the world

I am clearly

Madly in love

(with you)

It had a little impact
and then it had some more
An overwhelming feeling
impossible to ignore

It had a little impact
more than ever felt before
A huge impact on her heart
that was impossible

(to ignore)

Some things do, and some things don't. Some things will, and some things won't! We aren't always aware of what will and won't significantly affect us! It often all depends on timing. On synchronicity!

When a collision impacts you in a big way, it can feel like this crash has come out of nowhere! You're left startled and wondering where it, or they, came from; how did something so small affect you on such a big scale?

Sometimes, the minor things can make the most significant impact; it depends on how fast it travels and how far! Everything we do affects someone somewhere.

So it's essential to make sure that the impact we have is always a positive one; adverse effects have a way of following us around for a lifetime!

It's hard to undo the damage once done!

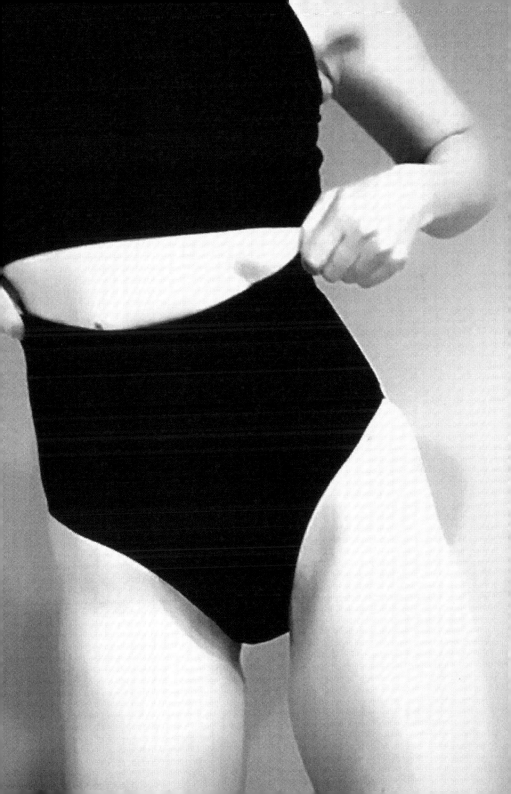

I wonder who you are with right now and who you were with yesterday. I wonder who has felt your touch and if you will kiss them in the same way.

I wonder how it feels for them. I wonder how it feels for you. I wonder if it feels the same with all, or whether there is someone special.

I do.

I wonder who else
has felt your lips
and if they felt
the same as on mine

I wonder who else
has felt your touch
and if they dream
of you all the time

(like I do)

It was the moments

between the moments

you never left deliberately

A space that always felt

like the most meaningful

synchronicity

(between us)

A certain amount of tension and pain is required to grab our attention, motivate us and give us the necessary energy to complete specific tasks! We communicate urgency to our mind and body that something needs doing. But too much tension in the body or mind for long periods can be unhealthy and begin to make us feel uncomfortable! If sustained for too long, it can make us want to run away and disconnect completely.

We often associate tension with pain and unconsciously steer away from it rather than into it. The way to deal with anxiety is to recognise what is creating it to dissolve it slowly. We are not supposed to feel tension for a sustained period. We also need to relax! When we are relaxed, we can live more freely, think more clearly, love more intimately, and speak more openly.

We all need space to breathe! If you find that peace and synchronicity with another, you will never feel that the space is left deliberately.

And we wonder about all of the uncertainties and all of the what-ifs in this world!

But we need to try and live and love 'in the moment' and do our best to try and not think too far ahead.

To try and enjoy our life in the 'here and now' and be grateful for the times that we feel love and the times we feel at peace.

Heavy is
this feeling
the closer
we become

With the weight
of expectations
knowing you
are the only one

(for me)

Sometimes the wait of time becomes so heavy that you feel weighed down by the anxiety of living too far in the future. Hoping the waiting will be worth it, and your patience will prove itself to be a positive partner in your life. You follow the light, the one that keeps reminding you of your worth— the one who fills you with hope and with words that make you shine. Like a beacon, it calls to you and encourages you to keep putting one foot in front of the other and reminds you never to lose sight of where or who you want to be. The light is there to help you see your path and to help you find your way. Find your light source and follow it, whoever, or whatever. It will guide you home.

I want to wake

with you today

tomorrow and

forevermore

So when I open my eyes

you are always

the first person

that I

(reach for)

We often think of yearning as a burning desire to have what we do not, but it can also be a yearning or longing to keep hold of and not lose what we already have. Whatever the case may be, our aspirations and desires are essential, as they continually inspire us, drive us onwards and keep us motivated and focused on the task at hand.

We also require lust and constant longing to keep the flame alight, to keep the passion flowing, and to keep us going essentially! I'd rather live in hope or hunger for the rest of my life than feel that I have it all. I can't imagine having it all is a great place to be!

The things you try when you are alone, wondering how it might turn out. But just when you think you might succeed, you hit a roadblock once again. You can't do it. You curse and cry and wonder if it's fear holding you back! Or perhaps a lack of courage? So you try again and again and again until you're feeling exhausted and crying and wondering why is it that you can't do it. Not today anyway. Not tonight.

So you give up safe in the knowledge that there is always tomorrow. Tomorrow will always offer another chance. Another opportunity to try again, and this time you will hopefully succeed. So you go to sleep with the resolve that you will try again tomorrow. And then tomorrow arrives, and you wake up early before the rest have risen from their rest, and your first thought is to wonder if today is the day. A mixture of hope and fear settles in once again. Good morning world. Will I succeed today? Let's hope so!

I feel a sickness
that's felt at sea

The waves are
breaking inside

(of me)

Contained, restricted, controlled and possessed. How does love feel when it is truly expressed? Is it demanding and dictated, or peaceful and free? Does it love the sum of my parts or only some parts of me?

Support and encouragement, or rules and regulations? Obsession and possession, or wonder and admiration? Can you see what love should undoubtedly be?

I can only explain it as the moment that one feels genuinely free, with another!

Some people are always seeking, and no matter how long they look or how far they travel, what they are looking for will always be out of reach. Why? Because what they are seeking is not outside of them. What they are seeking is not found in other people or by escaping to faraway places. Travelling is fun, and wealth brings many opportunities to do so. But if we do not like who we are, then no amount of travelling or money will ever fill that void. We will never find happiness in another if it is not within us. You are your saviour. You do not need someone else to tell you what you are worth or that you're doing okay.

The happiest people practice gratitude daily. They are kind, and their actions match their words. They seek and aspire, but they understand that everything they need is already within them. These are the dreamers. The poets. The philosophers. The sages. The muses. The ones who can take you to faraway places with their words. With their souls. With thoughts that fill your mind with inspiration and pure beauty. Let them take you there. Let them help you dream. We all deserve to dream. So dream big.

If truth be known

and truth be told

it is plain to see

when a heart is sold

Given to the one

who has let me be free

Given to the one

who truly understood

(me)

Here it was

so clear to see

I knew now how love

was meant to be

Not a hope

not a wish

not a desperate plea

It was pure

it was peaceful

it was always

feeling free

(beside you)

And you have

taught me more

than I knew

I needed to know

You have shown me

how love is in

the longing and

the constant flow

(between us)

I would rather feel the daily yearning and the constant longing than feel full or satisfied. I do not wish for unending joy or eternal bliss. I prefer to embrace the disappointments and let myself cry. So that when I finally reach my goals, I can genuinely rejoice in these precious moments and feel relatively satisfied.

The constant ebb and flow between having and not having is the nature of desire. Some days will end without fulfilment and satisfaction, yet we know there will be other days where the opposite will be true. Our desires continue to challenge us to achieve bigger and better things and to help us make our dreams come true!

Every unexpected turn

Every obstacle along the way

Every challenge overcome

made our love grow stronger

(every day)

'Que sera sera, whatever will be will be!' I love this saying! It reminds me to accept that there are some things we cannot change or force. When faced with unwelcome detours, it's easy to let the frustration we feel take control of our thoughts. And although we may wish for things to happen differently, or for people to be ready when we are, or for them to see things from our point of view, the reality is that some people may never be willing, or want to change or to see the world through our eyes. So we must accept that we can't always find a solution to every problem, but we can always dig deeper to find the resilience and the determination to keep going! To keep the faith and not give up!

This life is not easy, but no one ever promised it would be. The good things in life are often worth it and are invariably worth waiting for or fighting for; I am learning to evolve to be more patient by developing new strategies to help me wait. Restrictions and control build greater resilience and a fighting spirit that will help us overcome all the disappointments, frustrations and challenges we face now and in the future. The more obstacles we encounter, the more creative and imaginative we must become. I'm using this time to fire up my imagination and think of new ways to tackle every new problem that I encounter. As my desire grows, so does my determination.

From my eyes they come

as I let myself go

I feel you

touching me

as I let them flow

I've reached the point

of such joyful bliss

as I think of you

and the way

you always kiss

(me)

Tears of joy. Tears of relief. Tears of achievement. Tears of success. Experiencing such pleasure that we are so overwhelmed with happiness that such events can bring us to tears! Tears not of pain or suffering. But tears cried as a final release of all we have worked hard for, feared, or desperately wanted to achieve.

Tears cried as a release for all that might have been holding us back from living a whole and happy life. The ones that flow when we let love into our life. When we give ourselves over to the feeling, it frees our soul. These are the moments of joyful bliss when it feels as though our souls are crying their tears of joy for us.

As Alan Watts says, "I am throwing the ball away from me. I am embracing self-abandonment to be free". We can only truly love when we let go of the idea that love is about getting someone to love us. Love is merely loving your 'self' and loving others. That is all!

A line drawn

from A to C

and another drawn

from B to D

A universal symbol

A universal sign

of love

of one's affection

in just two lines

(X x)

We use emojis to help convey the meaning of our words, using them alongside our words or in isolation as a quick response to communicate to the other person how we are feeling. I find emojis very helpful in interpreting intent, particularly when we can't always look into the eyes and see for ourselves.

But of all the emojis and symbols I use, the one I still reserve for those I love is the simple cross! The universal sign of the kiss. The universal sign of love. It was yesterday that I'll remember, and today that you will see how much those four strokes you gave me really meant to me!

Irresistibly charming

without ever trying to be

Replying and responding

in a way that always

made me

(smile)

Letting

Our

Vulnerability

Exist

What is love

but...

The joy in the wanting
The ache in the longing
The pleasure in the anticipating
And the peace found in the knowing

that there is no place
you'd rather be...

Often the young can speak such truth. I was driving my daughter to ballet class recently when she looked at me earnestly and said, 'You know mummy, some boys just want to make you sad, and that's bad!' I looked at her and smiled and said, 'You're absolutely right, beautiful, and between you and me, I still have no idea why some of them want to. But even though some will want to make you sad, some boys will only want to see you smile. But this is when they are no longer boys, my darling; this is when they have finally matured into men! These are the ones that you should want to see again and again!'

.

What is everything to you? Is it all that they say? Is it all that they do? What does true love feel like for you? Is it the feeling you get when you both embrace? Is it the look in their eyes or their beautiful face? Love is not as complex as we make it out to be. But this is what it truly feels like to me! We become one when I kiss you long, even though this love story has just begun. It's how you move, the rhythm in your bones, the look in your eyes, and how I always feel like I am home when I am with you.

There are a million ways to show you, but I need only show you one, for when you look into my eyes, you'll see my heart it is you've won.

It started with a feeling; it began with just a look; it started with an opened door and a photo that we took. It started when I whispered, I like you, I really, really do. It began when you told me, come here; I really like you too!

But it was not simply what you said; it was more about how you looked at me; it was the fire you lit inside when we exchanged our energies.

Cold metal on my hand

a push upon your door

A world of possibilities

was all I was looking for

Reckless, but with purpose

I came looking, for I knew

I would surely fall in love

the very moment

I saw how you

(looked at me)

If I drew you

as a flower

a beautiful dandelion

you would be

A wish come true

a chance I took

when you gave

your love

(to me)

Unsought

Unintended

Yet,

I would search

if I knew

There was

a chance

or a hope

that I would

find you

(again)

It was a moment of serendipity, a fairytale come true! Good luck and good fortune the day that I met you.

Often we discover things by chance. They make an appearance when we least expect it, and usually when we are not looking for them! A sliding doors moment, perhaps!

Do you wonder where you would be if that moment had never happened? If you'd said no instead of yes. If you had played safe, never tried, or believed that what you deserved was the best!

A strong man will always handle a woman with great care, even when the passion is overflowing. It is this deftness of touch that we all long for so much! When you find a man with worthy hands, you will understand what it feels like to be genuinely touched both on the outside of you and deep within. Where their fingers seem to reach much further than simply your skin, and hands that go deep and so far down into your soul, carrying it skilfully but without control. I always feel free when you are holding me.

With the greatest care
and such deftness of touch
your hands knew how
to leave me wanting so much

(more of you)

I want to come live

in your world

I want to see the

things you see

I want to see it all

through your eyes

I want to be

where you will be

(forevermore)

If we convey so much more through body language than our words, how absurd is it that we rely so much on the written word! I am of the generation of women who prefer to send video rather than text messages. I want to show you my face. I want you to see how I feel. I want to let you all know that the person you are talking to is real.

I like to tell you stories when I'm out, in my car, on my bed, or in the garden. I always like to look someone in the eyes, hear their tone of voice, and see their smile, or perhaps even their tears. I want to feel what they feel, and I also want to use my ears! I love voices, and I enjoy looking at others. I'm not one to connect deeply with someone without seeing them in person. I need physicality for all sorts of reasons.

But it's not just the embrace; it's more about seeing their face! I need to look at a face to see how it feels. When we look into their eyes, it starts to feel real! And all I ever see is the way that you are looking back at me!

You embrace me
without touching
You move me
without words

You love me
without needing
what you give
to be returned

(to you)

I can still taste your embrace

it's smooth texture

it's sweet flavour

But I dare not swallow

until I've had the chance

to savour

(all of you)

I like to cook, and I enjoy eating. But mostly, my enjoyment of food comes from the food's preparation. I love standing over the hob and breathing in the aromas of the evening's cooking. I find it relaxing and rewarding knowing that I'll be rewarded for my efforts. It's all in the cooking. It's the same when eating. Some things are best chewed slowly or swirled around in our mouth until the full flavour is absorbed.

I never like to eat too quickly. I'm never in a rush when it comes to food. I want to feel the texture and taste the flavour, and I always prefer a smooth and peaceful pace when it comes to relationships too. Relationships that go hard and fast die much more quickly than those that go slow and steady! The hare never won the race; the tortoise did. So slow and steady it is, savouring every mouthful as I go. The fun is in the tasting, not the swallowing! The joy is in the journey, not in the finishing!

It was a late-night amongst others, and your arms were holding me, and for the first time in a long while, I felt no desire to be free. At that very moment, I knew that this was where I wanted to be. It was a feeling only you, and I could feel, yet, everyone else could see; that we were in love.

I did not shrink myself smaller

to avoid an unwelcome embrace

I did not shrink myself smaller

to gain some extra space

I felt myself grow, to fill

the space between you and me

I felt for the first time, in a while,

in your arms is where I wanted

(to be)

I purse my lips together

trying to keep this love within

but out pops the little breath

that I try constantly to hold in

It makes the sweetest sound

like a sort of lovestruck lullaby

It's a song that my heart sings

but escapes as a little sigh

(only for you)

Oh, it's the sweetest sound that seems to escape from me. A simple sound but filled with so much complexity. It's a sound I've not heard from my heart before. It's a sound that I keep wanting to hear more and more.

When someone can make me feel the way you do, it must be the reason I'm always left wanting you. Who makes your heart sing? Who loves your everything? Love is a tapestry for sure! It's what we are all looking for!

I feel it rise from my chest and ignite all my nerves, a tingle, a sensation that straightens my curves. It makes me stand to attention until the feeling has gone, but when I feel it retreat, I always try to hold on... a little bit longer.

It may seem like a small gesture to some. It may seem like it's not a big deal to others. But being proud of the person you love and being proud to show them off is one of the biggest compliments you could receive from the one you love.

When we are happy to reveal who it is that we love. When we choose to acknowledge who it is, that matters to us publicly. For me, it is the most honest and authentic display of love and affection that one could make.

We know how important it is to show, not tell, as writers. So it follows that nothing matters more than what we do. Our actions will always, always speak louder than our words.

Being publicly

acknowledged

by you

was the most

romantic thing

you could

ever do

(for me)

Oh, little green light, why do you taunt me so? For every time I see you, it makes my heart go... BOOM!

Just a little light
that turns to green
Just a simple sign
every time it's seen

Oh, how I long for
your digital embrace
every time I see
you're in cyberspace

(I love you. I do)

My social media followers have often asked me if I feel what I write, and my answer is, of course, I do. I write for myself and self-expression, but I like to also share my words publicly for all to see, for others to feel my words' authenticity and share my vulnerabilities. And to know that they are crafted and composed from my heart.

Yet, it is not simply my words I want to impart. It's my story, and it's my life that I want to share with you. It's the only way I know how to write, the only way I want to. So maybe I'm not a writer. Perhaps I'm just me. But writing is the one thing I have found that has always helped me feel free!

Backspace is my friend
when I am writing to you
knowing the words that I say
I may have no chance to undo

So I only write from the heart
and only say what I feel
as I find it hard to pretend
and impossible to conceal

(how much I love you)

I stare in wonder

I stare in awe

at a love so real

at a love so raw

A dream I once had

a dream come true

the day, the moment

I laid eyes on you

(I love you)

When we stare in wonder when we stare in awe, it's that moment you realise that this is what you've always been looking for; a huge rush of happy hormones that make all your hairs stand on end. A wide-open mouth moment that you never want to end. Awe and wonder are emotions we rarely feel, yet they bring such a massive range of health benefits.

Often we can be so busy with our daily routines we forget to take ourselves out of our everyday lives to seek wonder and awe. We do not need to travel to experience awe necessarily. We do not need to stand in front of impressive monuments and wonder at the feats of humanity. We need only to look up at the sky or perhaps into another's eyes to see that wonder and awe exists everywhere!

The more I age, the less I feel the need to smile, and the more I allow myself to show others how I genuinely feel. Many people feel uncomfortable when they see someone unhappy or upset. But as I sat down and explained to my daughter and her friend when they were both upset, after having had two days of fun together, it was that it's perfectly okay to be sad. It's natural sometimes to feel miserable and tired and fed up and disappointed or annoyed or possibly even angry. It's normal to feel this way occasionally, as feelings come and feelings go.

My point to them both was to feel it, acknowledge it, and then let it go. I like to post pictures that show my full range of emotions, not just happy ones. It's never wrong to feel a certain way, as we sometimes need to feel sad before feeling happy again. Because just like the stock market, our feelings will always fluctuate.

And your beauty

was found

and your magic

uncovered

with every word

every smile

and every thing

I've discovered

(about you)

Revealing our true selves by allowing people to see where our magic comes from might feel a little like we are giving away our deepest secret. But a magician's magic is not just about the wonder of how they did the trick. It is about the performance and the showmanship that captivates you and slowly reels you in; it's akin to the magic you see when you look into the eyes of the ones you love. It's hard to disguise mutual attraction. It's hard to deny the chemistry. Some people are like exquisite art pieces; it is almost impossible to take your eyes off them, for there is always so much more to see, so much more to explore. They somehow keep you coming back for more.

People frequently like to ask couples how they met. What were the chance circumstances of their first encounter? Did you meet at work, or on a night out, or did mutual friends introduce you? Was it an instant attraction or more of a slow burn? A passionate embrace or perhaps a reserved first date? At what point did you know they were the right one for you? Love at first sight, or did it take years before it felt right?

How did your present or past love story begin? Do you believe you need to feel that fire within from the start? Or are you happy to wait for the spark to ignite later in the relationship? Which one was it for you? Did your perfect love story ever come true? Or is there someone still out there who is still waiting for you?

Our love story began
like most love stories do
grabbing your attention
and slowly hooking you

You kept turning my pages
and I kept turning yours too
It was a love story of fiction
yet this time, it was true

(I love you)

We all need to be acknowledged. In business, we expect it, and some almost demand it, but it is even more critical in our intimate relationships. Whether publicly or privately, being recognised helps boost our confidence and self-esteem. It makes us feel valued and that we matter, that we are worthy. Never underestimate the value of perhaps a like or a comment or even a private DM that acknowledges you and your existence here on earth. The acknowledgement helps to drive up our feeling of worth.

I am not talking about recognition and waxing lyrical about someone's achievement, which may come across as insincere, particularly if they only acknowledge you for their financial gain. I am not talking about calling someone a legend or a superstar! Because let's face it, these terms are only really for those who do incredible things and are genuinely worthy of that title!

I am talking about simple acknowledgement. Just a thank you to a kind comment or a simple smile to a stranger in the street. I'm not suggesting we need constant validation by others to determine our worth. But simply that we treat others with compassion, and we can do this by making sure they are "seen."

Some people intuitively always know what to do without you needing to tell them. It's as though they've taken the time to learn your language of love and can sense what it is you need. Or perhaps they always seek understanding first and know that the best way to love someone is to understand how they like to be loved.

Some people are easy to get from the get-go, and others take a lot of unwrapping. Multidimensional people that have layer upon layer that needs revealing. But with every discovery and every new layer is another welcome surprise. Their complexity is the attraction, and their depth makes you want to dive in and discover what mysteries lie beneath the surface.

Love is an adventure that we should take our time to explore. Love will always be the one that will keep you coming back for more.

You seem to

speak my language

and always intuitively

know what to do

Yet underneath

every new layer

will be another

surprise that is waiting

(for you)

I wish to write you a letter

of two pages

or maybe three

seal it tightly in a bottle

then trust it to the sea

I'd tell you what it felt like

what it felt like to be me

a dreamer who believed

that you and I were

(meant to be)

I clench my teeth together
as I feel a tingle down my spine
a multiple chemical reaction
every. single. time.

(I think of you)

I keep dreaming
I'm climbing down holes
wanting to explore
and even though
they are deep
I am not frightened
anymore

(because of you)

You made me high

You made me low

You took me where

I asked to go

You kept it real

You kept it fun

That's how I knew

you were the one

(for me)

We exist in this world in a state of constant highs and lows. It's the ebb and flow of how life and love go—riding high then feeling low. But sometimes, it's where we need to go. Wanting a life where our emotions are always at equilibrium is ignoring the needs of our natural state of being. We are designed to feel the highs, just as we are the lows. When we recognise that the lows serve a purpose, we start to let our feelings come and go as they please. Being stuck in the middle is no place to be. And that's why I love you, and you love me! These feelings we felt came with such intensity! If it's not a little bit frightening, then perhaps there are clouds but no lightning!

When we take our time and savour the moment, we give ourselves time to explore the full flavour of someone. To try and taste the parts of them that may go unnoticed if we choose to swallow them too fast. When we take a moment to see all the delicate flavours that exist alongside the stronger ones, we start to appreciate them for all of the ingredients, subtle or not so subtle, that go into making them taste as good as they do. It's only by knowing their full flavour that you can genuinely say, 'I love you.'

I try to sip you slowly

so your full flavour

I can explore

but the moment that I taste you

it always leaves me

wanting so much more

(of you)

If you have to keep a love hidden, is it truly love? If you cannot share your passion for this person with the world, can it ever be true if it is not there for all to see it in plain view? If you love someone, let them know, but if you need to keep them a secret, then perhaps you should let that love go. It's essential to feel like you are important to one another. How do they or you go about doing that? By allowing each other to be seen and allowing each other to acknowledge your love openly.

They should be proud of you and feel privileged to be recognised by you, and you should be proud of them and feel privileged to acknowledge them too. It's worth thinking about if this is not the case. Why hide you? What is it that they are protecting? An emotionally mature and healthy person treats you with the respect you deserve.

I'll never hide

my love for you

as you never hide

your love for me

It is always

in plain view

as we prefer for

everyone to see

(who it is we love)

It really is quite

something

when you feel it

you just know

It is something that

is so rare

that you simply

cannot let it go

(I love you)

You know it's something when it lights a fire in your soul. When it keeps replaying in your head, it makes you want to jump out of your bed and get going! Where it sends a shiver down your spine, and you can't help but think about it all the time! And when you feel it, you know that you cannot let it go this time! It is not the power of positive thinking, a healthy mindset, writing in a journal, or chanting daily affirmations. It is not reading inspirational quotes or serious self-talk! It is something altogether more wonderful!

It is love! And love conquers all! Love is the one thing that makes us strive to be the very best we can be. Love is the one thing that will genuinely make us happy! Don't talk yourself out of it or believe it is something you do not need. Love is the MOST beautiful thing this life of ours has to offer. We can live with very little, just as long as we have love

These are strange times with a lot of bewilderment, making it much more challenging to know what is real and what is not. Being held hostage over your health and fellow humans has a significant effect on our emotional wellbeing. Applauding some and mocking or judging others seems to be the order of the day. We are all heroes. We are all doing our part. We do not need to come out of this collective trauma more resilient, with any more skills, with more appreciation for life, with a desire to travel more, with needing to love more, or even with more humility!

Hopefully, some of us will come out of this as survivors in every sense of the word! Physically, mentally, financially and perhaps spiritually. It's easy to be held hostage emotionally in these strange times. But you have a right to feel down and find captivity emotionally draining. Everyone's experience differs depending on their individual circumstances. It's easy to judge others when you have a fridge full of food, an income stream still coming in, and your biggest concern is when you will next be able to visit the hairdresser. The only thing we need to come out of this with is a little bit more empathy. I acknowledge you!

I acknowledge you

You acknowledge me

This is the only potential

I will ever need to see

There is part of me

that wants it to stay

but another part of me

that wants it to go

It's the kind of feeling

that makes me so high

but also a feeling

that can make me so low

(is it love?)

There is more

to explore

and much

more to see

There is more

to you

and so much

more to me

(let's go)

We recognise that we are emotionally healthy when pursuing genuinely good things for ourselves and others. People who inspire us. Who are kind and loving and not spiteful, jealous or resentful, and who genuinely have our best interests at heart. We all know that ultimately what we seek, we will find. If we haven't seen it, we may be looking in the wrong places or searching for something we think we want, but we likely desire something else a little more.

Everything comes at a cost. Ultimately there is no right or wrong in who we choose to be or what tasks we wish to do. But look at what motivates you. What comes to you effortlessly, and what is the most rewarding. There is no point in having material wealth if, emotionally and spiritually, we are poor. It is all about what we wish to be remembered for. I hope I am remembered for loving endlessly and not simply for what I have done, but how I have accomplished it.

With your help, I am learning to exhale. Slowly. Deliberately. Counting the seconds as every last bit of air slowly leaves my lungs. Trusting there will always be more to fill them up again. And trust that you will never ask me to hold my breath but leave me ample space to breathe. To explore the endless possibilities; to think; to create; to love; to grow; to expand; to reflect; to just be.

So much can be accomplished when we become much more aware of our breath. When we make an effort to slow things down, we start to see there is no finish line. There is no race. We are space. We are meant to explore. This is what we are here for.

With a chance

to breathe

I am starting

to see

in between

the spaces

you leave

the endless

possibilities

(of you and I)

There is something so romantic about receiving a letter:
the anticipation, the wait and the not knowing what the
subsequent communication will bring. Will your friend
feel the same, or perhaps things will have changed. What
news will come this time? Good or bad? Happy or sad? As a
child, I had a pen pal who lived in America. We'd send each
other all sorts of beautiful things. Things that we had made
or bought for each other. I spent hours recording particular
messages on tape on my pink tape deck in my bedroom. I'd
send these tapes to her with little gifts and handwritten notes.
The anticipation was terrific. I loved receiving trinkets from
her, as did she from me.

I can't remember when we stopped, but one day we did.
It might have been because I was so busy with ballet and

school that I no longer had time. But it was a wonderful part of my childhood. Communication now is so instantaneous that it leaves little to the imagination - there is hardly any anticipation. Today's communication relies on self-control. Not allowing yourself to say too much, but just enough and only every so often. I love the experience and whole romance of just a few pertinent words. At this precise point, life feels a little like wartime, only that we deal with an invisible enemy. So perhaps now is a good time to bring back the love letter. This instant communication has a way of killing romance. I wish there were a way to get it back. I really do.

Romantic notes have a unique way of communicating that they love you.

I am trying hard to
pace myself with you
so that I will always
feel my breath

Yet, as slowly as I go
the very thought of you
always leaves me

(breathless)

I've always believed that if we cannot feel our breath, we are moving too fast. It's a sign that we need to slow down and become more mindful and purposeful in what we do.

When I feel anxiety (or even excitement) creep up on me, I notice a rapid change in my breathing. My heartbeat quickens, and I'm either feeling very high or downright terrified. Either way, it can leave me feeling breathless and sometimes giddy.

When I start to lose my breath, I look for things to do that require my utmost attention, activities that will slow me down and bring me back down to earth.

I started learning the art of origami during the lockdown, as it requires a tremendous amount of patience and precision to be able to turn the ordinary into the extraordinary. It's all in the doing, not in the done. It is choosing quality over quantity every time.

If something is worth doing, it's worth doing well. This goes for relationships too. Think of everything that you write or say as being stored away in a journal to be read by either of you one day. You may just be a little more mindful of your words.

Always try to make them purposeful and beautiful. Everything is a creation. We are what we create.

I wish my words

would land more slowly

taking their time to cross the seas

Flying gracefully through the air

taking in the beautiful scenery

Weaving their way to you slowly

making you wait so patiently

And when they arrive

you'll know they're from me

when you see there are

only three words for you to read

(I love you)

Return you know it will; I believe it always does—the feeling of falling, so spectacularly in love. One of the greatest feelings in the world, and often when we feel our most alive, is when we feel the heady heights of infatuation and the beginning of a powerful passion with another. This desire to know someone inside out can be all-consuming, and it can sometimes feel that it is taking over our lives.

Sometimes, the only way to cope with the intensity of these emotions is to pull away and hope that with time and some self-restraint, we can manage this feeling of wanting them to become more familiar. It's scary putting your heart on the line with the possibility you will end up hurt. It's even unnerving wondering whether it will ever happen to you again.

But I can promise you it will happen again, for it always does. Love is not linear; it goes round and round. There is enough love out there for everybody. You have to believe. When you start to believe that it is everywhere, you no longer wish for it to stay.

Lying around the corner

I believe it will always be

The feeling of the falling

in love so spectacularly

In the wanting

I am happy

In the busy

I am content

In the waiting

I am trusting

in the promises

of your intent

Patience is a virtue, and as a fellow poet said in his comment to me the other day, 'the wisdom is in the waiting... a lot of life seems to be about being a good wait-er... who we are in the wait.'

His words resonated with me and made me think about why we are finding it increasingly more difficult to wait as a society, delay our gratification, and leave our desires unfulfilled until the time is right.

Why do we persist in having things now? Why do we insist on consuming a vast amount of precious resources to fulfil our desires and every whim with little consideration of the consequences of this behaviour on future generations? Why is convenience food more important than the plastics that fill our oceans, and our desire to be seen in the latest fashions or with the newest handbag more important than sustainability and recycling? Why are we so unhappy waiting when uncertainty and unpredictability are what makes life so exciting?

I'm happy in the wanting. I'm content in the busy. I am trusting that the waiting will be worth it in the end. I trust in you. I trust in your intentions. Being a good wait-er is more satisfying than you might realise. We can find just as much joy in the anticipation, in our unfulfilled desires.

I have faith in you
I have faith in me
What I love is unknown
What I love I can't see

Still, I know what I want
and what I want is you
I believe I deserve
for you to love me too

When I say I want to 'see' you, it comes from wanting to be closer to you. But it also comes from the desire to know more about you. There is so much of 'you' that I want to explore. But even without knowing you, I can still love you, as I know that I too deserve that same sort of love. This faith in others and love for someone I don't 'know' makes me appreciate that I am becoming a fully realised person. I know what I want in life. I know what makes me happy. And I am delighted to pursue it.

Success is following your passion. Success is doing what you want to do. So if I say 'I love you,' which I just have. It does not come from knowing you. It comes from a place of believing that you are worthy of my love. Thank you for letting me in. Thank you for giving me time. Thank you for reading my words and feeling what I feel. I am truly grateful.

I can see myself when I look at you. In your eyes, I now see what you can see too. A reflection of all that you see in me. A clue, an idea, of your reality. It is this that I love. It is this that I crave. It is seeing the way that you look at me each day.

You can tell a great deal from the way someone looks at you. It is difficult to know what another is thinking or how they feel, but the clue, the truth, lies within their eyes. Who are we, but what someone else can see? Who you are perceived to be is modelled in another's mind as their reality. It is their perception and their truth. All that they know and don't know about you.

Look at you...
So I looked at me
but I could not see
what you could see

But when I looked at you
as you looked at me
in your eyes I saw
what you could see

(in me)

We said

very little

our eyes

said a lot

A mutual

understanding

language

forgot

(I hear you)

We rely on language to close geographical distances and connect with those that matter. Still, when we are in the company of the people that we have a real, immediate or intimate connection, language becomes superfluous.

"I see all I need to see and hear all I need to hear without you saying a word. I know what matters to you, and you know what matters to me."

When you connect on the same level, there will be a mutual understanding that needs never to be spoken aloud.

Love will never rain; it will only ever pour and always make
you feel an unquenching thirst for more. Soaked in sensuality
and drenched in desire, there's an energy for you, which
never seems to tire. Consumed by you, but still hungry for
more. Love never rains; it only ever pours.

How can it be

that I see

you everywhere

It seems that

everything

reminds me

(of you)

The mind can manifest feelings, but it cannot do this without seeing or visualising what it wants. The more we expose ourselves to the object of our desire, the stronger that desire grows. Familiarity can heighten feelings, and exposure can increase our desire.

We love the familiar almost as much as we love the new, just as we love having fun but love being good too. We have two minds because we are light and dark and night and day. So keep it fresh and keep it fun. We love the moon just as much as we love the sun.

They say love looks

not with the eyes

but with the mind

Yet, the moment

I laid eyes on you

I knew, I wanted you

(as mine)

The 'thinking mind' has a lot to answer for. It acts spontaneously, and it reacts to our feelings. When you reach your boiling point, make sure you turn down the heat to a simmer. It's never a good idea to cook things too quickly. A simmer will retain the flavour and help keep you in control.

Turn that 'observing mind' on and recognise when you're letting your emotions take over. It's easy to succumb, but it is much easier in the long term to let things happen naturally. If you struggle with what to say, maybe it is best not to say anything at all.

It's hard to know

just what to say

as you are

the only one

to ever make

me feel this way

(only you)

Oh, I do, I do, I do, I do, I do, I do! Why is it that when we are told not to do something, we end up more determined to do it? Often it's the case that the more we try to fight an emotion, the stronger it will become. Sometimes even though we try, there are forces beyond our control. Lust is such a force. In fact, it's the most potent force in the universe. The actual glue that binds a man and woman together. It's lust that creates desire, and it's lust that keeps it strong. Love is its poorer relation. We are so caught up in love, but the actual fire, energy and flames of passion come from lust. Sometimes we don't like the wanting, yet at the same time, we do. The wanting makes us take action, but it also creates an inner turmoil, a constant churning that drives us forward.

I don't want to want you like this

(but I do)

Do you wonder

what I wonder?

Where it wanders

where it goes?

Well, I'm imagining

and I'm dreaming

of a million scenarios

(with you)

Do you really want to know? Maybe not. After all, a vivid imagination is better than perfect memory. And it's way more fun and possibly more interesting if we fill in the blanks or recreate new scenes and scenarios, rather than relying on our memory of past events to keep us entertained. As wonderful it is to wonder and to wish, the only way to make wishes come true is to take serious action. Otherwise, we run the risk of it forever remaining a wish.

If you want something, you need to ask. If you desire something, then you need to take action. It may not turn out as you had hoped for, but it's better than doing nothing at all. Turn that thinking brain off and stop making excuses. As the catchphrase goes, 'If you can dream it, you can do it.' So just do it.

The days between

thinking about you

and not thinking

about you,

are getting smaller

(I think I love you)

When we consider something new, we often use the phrase that we are in 'two minds.' That's because we have two minds! In Zen, they refer to these two minds as the 'thinking mind' and the 'observing mind.' The 'thinking mind' is where we have incessant daily chatter. The 'thinking mind' can't be controlled, but we can tame it. How? By making sure we do not fuse the 'observing mind' with it. It needs to reign in the "thinking mind" like a parent does with a toddler throwing a small tantrum.

The trick is not to resist it but to realise that these intense emotions will come, but they will also go. But the more resistance we apply, the more it will take over our waking thoughts. It's okay to feel the intensity of the emotion, but fighting it will only make it stronger. So feel it, acknowledge it, but then let it go. All is well. Just enjoy life for the beautiful ride it is.

It's the way

that you smile

it's the joy

that you bring

It's the look

in your eyes

that means

everything

(to me)

The feeling never leaves

it simply refuses

to depart

You were a

one-way ticket

with a destination

to my heart

Our thoughts
control our desires
and our desires
our point of view.

Which is why it is
so pointless
trying to talk me
out of

(loving you)

What you desire will often be different to me. Add even
if we viewed the world similarly. It's difficult for me to see
what you will see, just like it is difficult for others to see what
makes me truly happy. Life is simply perspective and desire.
And our perspective will always be driven by our desires.
Because our thoughts control our desires and our desires
control our point of view.

I believe we can easily recognise love. Just like I believe in love at first sight? I can usually tell when two people are in love. You notice true love by how they both look at each other When one feels something so deep within, it is challenging to keep it in.

It is expressed through our eyes and felt through our gentlest touch. If you have to work at it, surely it can't be love. Love should never feel as if it needs to be fought for. Love is given freely. It is peaceful and calm.

When in love, our whole demeanour changes as we begin to experience the heady effects of the 'love drug' of oxytocin. We begin to feel less pain, and we start to feel almost invincible, as though the world is on our side. Love can make us see things in a much more positive light. It can help us get through even the most difficult of days.

I think you always thought; I think you always knew; I think you did believe that I would always fall in love with you.

I wonder if

you can tell

if you can see it

in my eyes

I wonder if

you can feel it

if you can easily

recognise

(love)

I want your messy

I want your soul

I want the 'you'

when you lose control

(I want rock n roll)

A terminal desire

and I'm looking

for some relief

For a heart that

has been stolen

by a beautiful

loving thief

Has love stolen anything from you? Your dreams, your hopes, your ambitions? It's easy to be swept away with the goals of another and forget that love can be a thief to your own dreams. It can leave you paralysed and focused only on your love interest and make you forget your own pursuits. It can make you choose love over everything else. It's not until the love departs or wanes that you become painfully aware of what you might have given up. What didn't you do as a result of your last relationship? What dreams and ambitions did you forget or put on hold for love?

Love is sometimes a thief. But love is also to be found in many people and many things. What do I love? Dancing, writing, listening to music, sunshine on my face, spending time with the people who make me laugh and people who bring me joy. It's all about the quality, not the quantity of these connections. And most of all, it's about prioritising yourself. Fall in love by all means, but also fall in love with you and your own dreams.

When we are missing someone or something, it's helpful to remember that nothing happens to us; it only occurs within us! We control what we choose to think and how we choose to feel. Over the last few years, some relationships have been strained from lack of, or too much, physical contact! What remains constant, though, is how one feels inside. How we choose to think is up to us. Whether our loved ones are near or far, they will travel with us wherever we are, if they stay within us. We will all be together again. In the meantime, let's keep those wonderful memories alive!

Even without you

I feel you are near

Even without you

I feel you are here

Within me, you stay

Within me, you are

Within me, you'll be

whether near

or whether far

(forever)

Oh, if I did not love you

so loved you would still be

as your beauty would stay

whether with, or without me

Oh, but love you, I do

and forever love you, I will

my muse and my lover

my heart you do fill

A thing of beauty is a joy forever.
Its loveliness increases; it will never
pass into nothingnes ...

John Keats

Beauty surrounds us in many noticeable and sometimes in not so many noticeable ways. The one constant thing, though, is that it still remains whether this beauty is admired or not admired. A thing of beauty cannot be changed. As Keats says, 'Its loveliness increases; it will never pass into nothingness.'

If we stay kind, no matter how many lines on our face or grey hairs on our head, our beauty will remain forever.

Hands crossed
upon my chest
I close my eyes
and let it rest

Courage matched
with real desire
my love for you
will never tire

The only thing I truly believe we need to be in life is brave. Brave enough to live. Brave enough to love. Brave enough to be strong. Brave enough to be kind. Brave enough to seek. Brave enough to find.

Our courage must be equal to our desire. Our efforts must be equal to our expectations. And although we feel we must continue to try our best and labour long and hard, there comes a time also when we must let it rest.

Treat love gently and just let it grow. Be brave enough to take it slow.

I'm not sure

if you feel it too

but it's a

constant ache

this wanting

(you)

Helping remove

a safety pin

is such an

ordinary

thing to do

but that night

I was intent on

trying my best

in removing it

(for you)

I'm not certain

why I recall it

why it is seems

so significant

to me

Perhaps it was

our togetherness

of both working

collectively

(to free you)

I've been called

so many names

more than just a few

But the only one I

hold onto is the one

that came from you

(I love you)

Move a little faster

or you'll be left behind

Move a little faster

you're running out of time

Time stands still for no man

It is not patient, it does not wait

So move a little faster

before it is too late

(and she's gone!)

Two words are all

you need to say

The first is

come

The second is

(stay)

We talk about the flowers

and the worms and the bees

We talk about our gardens

and about our apple trees

We talk about the small things

like freezing apple sauce

We talk because you love me

and I love you, of course

(I do)

'You're driving me wild!'

'Well, I'm glad I have a garden!'

Little moments that made me smile.

Conversations that have always been worth my while.

Cute emojis and the most perfect phrases, you are by far the sweetest man I have known in ages.

It does feel

as if you reach

down into my soul

in a way that

no one else can

Almost as if you

have a special key

that unlocks me

like no other man

It is easy to fall into relationships but much harder to drop out of them, especially when a connection becomes so strong and has existed for so long. As Adler states, 'all our problems are interpersonal. Ultimately, we live our lives for ourselves, yet we do not live by ourselves or only for ourselves. We exist as part of a community and a comprehensive social network'. Even though we are not living to satisfy other people's expectations, we still need to consider what is expected of us when it comes to being in any relationship.

For me, as Adler would agree, any relationship that imposes restrictions on another ultimately will fail or fall apart. Because what is not free cannot be called love. Control causes tension and oppression rather than peace and calm from a trusting and open relationship. When you love someone, you will care only for their happiness. Seeing them happy is the ultimate act of love. So set them free. Let love come freely, and it will find you.

I knew it would

never be easy

I always knew

the deeper we went

the harder it would be

as I became closer to you

and you to me

But you make me feel...

(so free)

I wish it to end

yet, I want it to stay

Torn in half

in the wanting

to go both ways

(with you)

Some things just aren't meant to be. It might feel like home, you might feel it in your bones, but it's just not your destiny. We blame timing, as though it has something to do with our decisions and choices. We believe that it might have worked if only we had more time, weren't so busy, had more resources, etc. But the truth is, perhaps it was never suitable for you, and your destiny was headed somewhere else.

Sometimes you've got to be brave enough to make a decision and simply stick with it. Being stuck in the middle will drive you crazy, torn between following your heart or following your head. Well, neither your head nor your heart should have the final say until your mind, body, and soul are thinking as one.

No one can interfere in this task; it is yours alone. No one can make this decision for you. Only you know what it is that you truly want. If you are really prepared to go for it, then go after it with everything you have!

Things take time. They require patience and faith that everything will eventually fall into place; if only we could just let things be and surrender ourselves to space. To realise that nothing can, nor should be contained or held onto.

There are moments we wish we could relive again, moments that may have passed too fast. Moments we genuinely want to last forever. But these moments move away from us swiftly into a brand new day. And although some moments may pass too soon, there are some moments we pray will end just as quickly.

Moments where we can avoid our current circumstances so that we might end up in a place where everything feels better, perhaps calmer and kinder. A place where we have space to breathe and time to think. Where there is less uncertainty and a lot less fear, and where everything feels a little safer. A kind of utopia where the dice we roll always falls on a double six!

But here we are, existing in this very moment. A reality that is simply you and me. So what do we do... what will we do today to make the very most of this moment? I guess the only thing that we can do! Which is not to waste a precious minute of our lives. Life is short. It's true.

But it is much shorter if you are not doing the very things you were always born to do.

I've put my faith in time

surrendering to space

Trusting that it will all

simply fall into place

(with you)

I wonder if there will ever be a day

where I will not think of you—

I see you everywhere

When I see people walk—

I only ever think of how you move

When I hear people talk—

I only ever hear your voice

I try and think of other things

but I only ever see your face

You are everywhere—

every place I ever go

I have found the switch

but I cannot turn it off

However, it is interesting how you do not feed into the societal norm of wanting to reciprocate with me. Perhaps you feel I have already attracted enough attention and applause, so I do not need any more from you! That I might lose your applause in the sea of noise, and I might then only see you as one of many.

So rather than clap for me, you stay silent. Because your silence is much louder, I can now hear you more clearly and listen to you more intently. I will notice you, and I do. But you have always stood out to me. Your silence was never necessary.

Because I have always loved you. X

People can

see it in me

and I too

can see

it in you

It's undeniably

a special place

so many want

to reach into

(oh, your eyes)

I try and push it back down

as I feel it rise up

This overwhelming feeling

that seems to never give up

I always feel it rise

when I think of you

It's the most wonderful feeling

being in love

(with you)

Love is straightforward. Mutuality and chemistry are everything. All we need to know is that they need us back.

needing me back

is all I need ask

(of you)

~ will it ever end?

poetry by YΛYΛ

In her debut book, Instagram poet, spoken-word performer, and visual artist, YAYA, has pulled together a beautiful collection of her favourite poems, commentary, and thoughts about life and love. Immerse yourself in her world for a moment or even for a while. But every picture and every thought is guaranteed to make you smile.

Printed in Great Britain
by Amazon

78340511R00199